SUBLIME HIDEAWAYS

Remote Retreats and Residences

gestalten

Pristine Seclusion: Finding Inspiration Beyond the City

In a world that has grown increasingly mapped, measured, and connected, technology has made it possible to live almost anywhere. Areas and spaces that once seemed forbidding now feel full of possibility—truly, we live in ways that few could have dreamed of only a decade ago. For as long as they have existed, cities have beckoned to us with their promise of excitement, autonomy, convenience, and opportunity, but in recent years more and more people are looking to escape them, settling—at least temporarily—in more remote locations. They are seeking good things: a stronger connection to the natural world, a slower and more intentional way of life, and a deeper connection to the people around them. Waking up to the sound of the Pacific Ocean, sharing a morning coffee with the tropical birds of Brazil's jungles, contemplating the rustling pine trees of the Karelian forest during a Zoom call, having dinner while catching the sun's last beams as it falls behind Tasmanian mountains, or stargazing from a moonlit mountain terrace—these are glimpses of a life one might lead when far from it all. Just as the stunning architecture showcased in the following pages highlights the otherworldly, captivating, and majestic natural surroundings, slow-paced living celebrates the things that are truly important—the people we love, the work we do, and our relationship with the environment.

From the stylish and calming interiors of the retreats featured in this book, one can observe the change of seasons, dramatic shifts in weather, and the cycles of local flora and fauna. Full of sunlight, designer furniture, and evocative artworks, these spaces are welcoming sanctuaries for their residents, where they find inspiration and focus. Home libraries and offices are perfect for those seeking quiet concentration, but a leisurely stroll through a lush rainforest, a swim in a pool overlooking the ocean, or a challenging hike up a misty mountain can also change one's perception and refresh one's outlook.

LEFT PAGE Remote residences offer a whole new level of presence and contemplation—close to nature, one can observe changes in seasons and cycles of local flora and fauna.

Located in some of the most picturesque spots around the globe, these contemporary hideaways meld modern aesthetics with setting-inspired forms, resulting in homes that blend with, augment, and look quite at home in their surroundings. Scattered across four continents—Europe, Australia, and North and South America—these permanent homes, secondary houses, and holiday rentals follow different styles and approaches, yet they are all founded on a commitment to sustainability and a deep relationship to nature.

When it comes to remote architecture, treating the location with respect becomes essential. Whether situated in the Australian desert or on a tiny Norwegian island, these off-the-grid homes are popping up in the most hard-to-reach places, with construction processes and building-material choices tailored to the local environment and its natural resources. This challenge has become a creativity booster for architects, inspiring design choices that display connections to traditional, even indigenous design practices.

For many decades, the residential architecture of masters like Ludwig Mies van der Rohe, Jørn Utzon, and José Antonio Coderch was considered an unattainable benchmark of excellence. Nevertheless, contemporary architects, including those found within this book, have consistently pushed boundaries, and have given us homes to rival those treasures of the previous century. While building upon the most striking design movements of the past, their works pose relevant, pressing questions, and make space for an evolving environmental consciousness.

Sublime Hideaways celebrates the dreamers who seek to explore life beyond the city. Filled with inspiring stories from around the world, it showcases stunning, tucked-away residences, from rustic mountain retreats to dreamlike beachside escapes. The book takes readers on a journey through creative and startling architecture, while pausing to consider each place's special, completely unique identity. It also peeks into the lifestyles of those who have made the leap to these far-flung places, and the inspiring atmospheres they have created there.

RIGHT PAGE Waking up to the sound of the ocean, sharing a morning coffee with birds, stargazing from a mountain terrace—these are just a few ways to spend time when far from it all.

Slow-paced living celebrates the things that are truly important—the people we love, the work we do, and our relationship with the environment.

Desert Hideaway Overlooking a Valley

HIGH DESERT RETREAT   AIDLIN DARLING DESIGN
PALM DESERT, CA, USA   2019

The desert—mysterious, dangerous, and beautifully desolate—might at first seem like a difficult place to thrive, and the landscape in and around California's Coachella Valley is no exception.

Yet some, who have come in search of crisp comfort, exhilarating quiet, and deep contact with the environment, have done exactly that.

Frankly speaking, the High Desert Retreat belongs to the desert only partly. Located on a rocky plateau outside the California town of Palm Desert, the house makes superb use of the landscape's inherent drama. Aidlin Darling Design, known for its ergonomic and mesmerizing projects, have with the High Desert Retreat created something of an oasis, a structure that feels both of the desert and other.

With a goal of adapting to the arid desert climate, and without removing a single Pinyon tree (a pine with a life cycle up to 600 years), Aidlin Darling Design created a modernist, single-story volume with a floating roof plane and open-air terrace pool. This is a single-family, three-bedroom secondary residence, with views of the Coachella Valley and San Jacinto Mountain Range, where one can enjoy the desert's mood swings and tranquil mountain light. Peculiarly shaped plants and boulders cover the grounds, whose shadows resemble mythical creatures when captured in the rectilinear spaces and diaphanous elements of the architecture.

Inside, the otherworldly magic continues. Wood, stone, and concrete follow the rhythm of the terrain outside, while offsetting its wilder nature with straight lines and smooth surfaces. The color palette becomes lighter, and the shapes become more playful. Designed to decrease the speed of living, the resort's spaces function as anchors, channeling the attention of their inhabitants into meditative processes like cooking, reading, sharing a meal, or conversing with a significant other. Thoughtfully chosen design objects and art pieces create vibrant accents to the otherwise calming palette, and complement the mountain and desert views.

LEFT PAGE The parallel walls of the open-air terrace swimming pool frame the captivating and stunning view of the Coachella Valley below.
RIGHT PAGE It was both architects' and residents' wishes to interfere with the natural landscape as little as possible and not remove any pine trees from the setting.

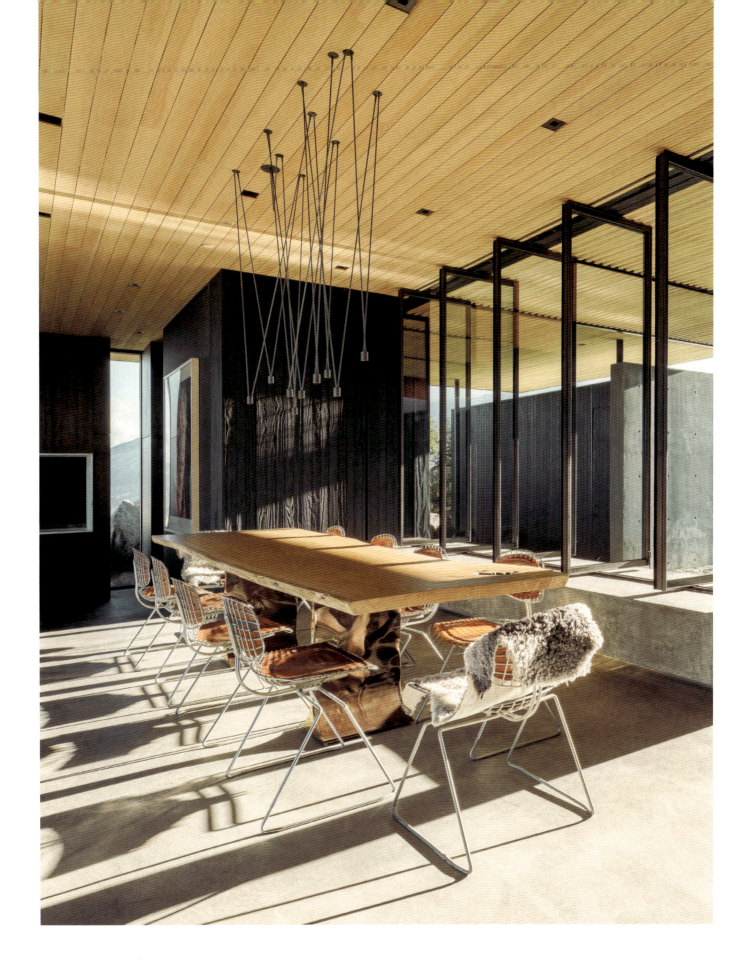

LEFT PAGE The projecting roof with a clear outline serves as a source of shade for sunny days spent outdoors by the pool. RIGHT PAGE Minimalist design of the dining table highlights the edgy features of steel chairs. FOLLOWING PAGES The spacious living area with a corner sofa, flooded with natural light, provides both a comfortable atmosphere and breathtaking views.

The rectangular shape of the bathroom maintains the graphic contours of the space, while the mesmerizing views of the desert serve as the main accents of the bath area. RIGHT PAGE The color palette of the interior draws its inspiration from the surrounding landscape and provides enough contrast to emphasize the border between the wild and the built.

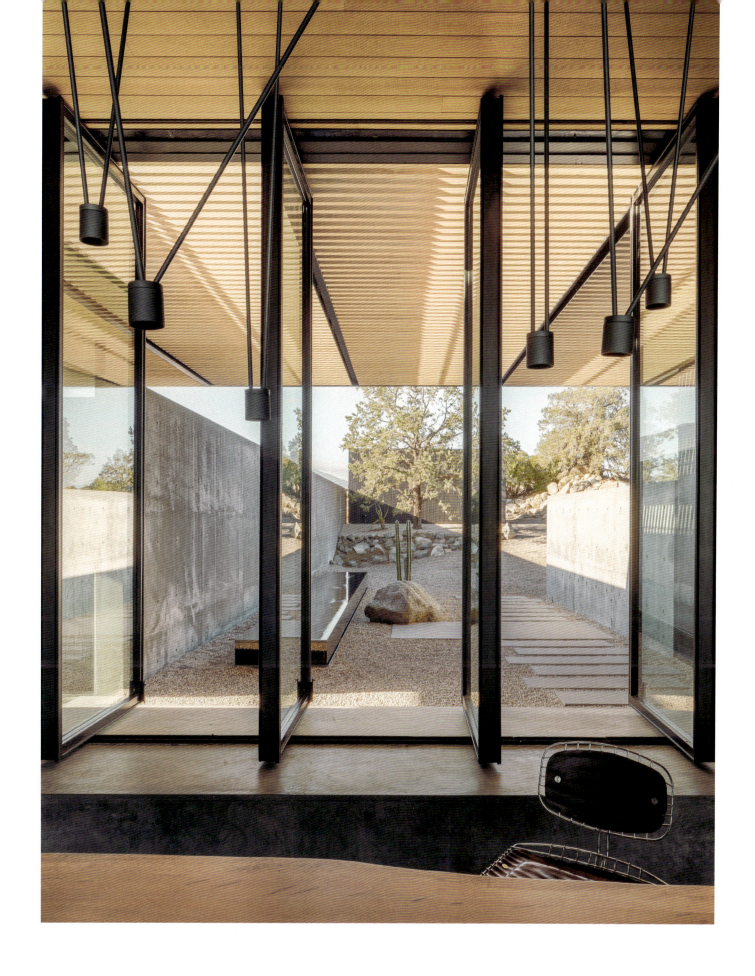

LEFT PAGE The luxurious and radiant accents of the artwork more than compensate for the subdued colors and comfortable textures of the interior.
RIGHT PAGE The wide open floor-to-ceiling windows blur the boundaries between inside and outside, making the home part of the surroundings.

LEFT PAGE Minimalist features, such as clean lines and unadorned surfaces, create a sense of unity between the built environment and the natural world. RIGHT PAGE The residence is imbued with a sense of magic during the golden hour, a time of day when the sun is low in the sky, and its rays take on a warm, golden hue.

A Dispersed Dream House in the Mountains

BALLEN HOUSE   LCLA OFFICE AND CLARA ARANGO
EL RETIRO, COLOMBIA   2021

Currently a secondary home, meeting place, and art residence for the local community, Ballen House, in El Retiro, Colombia, makes brilliant use of the steep slope on which it is built. Situated  6,890 feet (2,100 meters) above sea level, in a mountain meadow that was once a pasture for grazing cattle, the home shows the striking use of stainless steel and concrete, offering an unusual but perfect complement to the foggy, mysterious rainforest that surrounds it.

The house consists of two separate structures, connected by a path and a large garden whose orchids and bromeliads suggest a strange tropical zone high in the mountains. Oslo- and Medellin-based architecture and landscape studio LCLA Office, with the help of local architect Clara Arango, decided on a bifurcated design structure in order to create two distinct sensory experiences. Each structure has its own carefully curated garden, as well as its own unique relationship with the site: one is more grounded and earthbound, with a humid, even cave-like atmosphere, while the other is elevated, and feels more outward-looking and extroverted. Because the architects chose to use the same materials inside as well as out (making great use of layered concrete and stainless steel), each structure also has the feeling of being quite a bit larger than it actually is.

Despite their separation, these two structures behave as a single house, united by consistent interior design and a shared sense of aesthetics. The minimalist, precisely designed wooden furniture and cushioned concrete sitting spaces gesture toward classic Scandinavian design, while the spacious, panoramic windows delightfully spoil this visual asceticism, framing spectacular rainforest views that seem painted by a 19th-century Romanticist. Ultimately, Ballen House is a place that accommodates almost any kind of mood or point of view. Its volumes and gardens inspire both reflection and expression, and its design keeps it both grounded and in the clouds.

LEFT PAGE Large windows allow the lush forest trees to become a part of the interior.
RIGHT PAGE The concrete façades of the residence's architecture are integrated into the visual rhythm of the landscape design, complementing and enhancing each other.

LEFT PAGE Each of the two volumes of the residence has its own carefully curated garden, incorporating a variety of mountain plants to create a beautiful and inviting outdoor space. RIGHT PAGE Wooden surfaces and warm carpets make the minimalist interior cozy. FOLLOWING PAGES The green upholstery of the furniture is in harmony with the outside view.

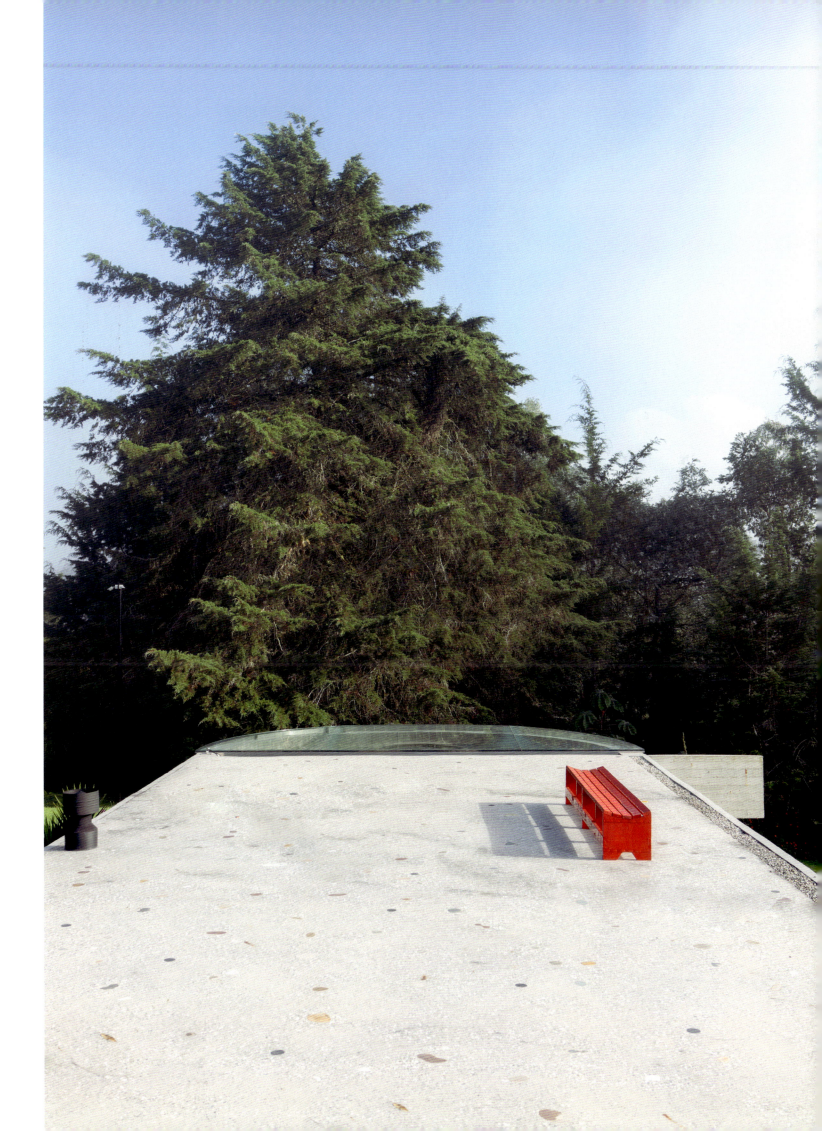

An Artful Hideaway on the Calmer Coast

HOBART HOUSE   HEARTH STUDIO AND MURRAY BARKER
WEST HOBART, AUSTRALIA   2018

A far cry from the rugged mountains and ancient pine forests of the West Coast, Tasmania's capital city of Hobart, nestled in the southeast, is home to much of the island's population. But, seek-

ing refuge from their home base in Melbourne, it was the sleepier suburb of West Hobart that photographer Lauren Bamford and musician Keith Mason chose for their getaway house. Hobart House (nicknamed Slow Beam by the owners) is a chic, two-story house situated on the fringe of a bush reserve, with views of River Derwent and South Hobart.

Hearth Studio, an interior architecture practice known for its sensitive and responsive projects, worked carefully to realize the couple's vision, creating a design at once dramatic, stylish, and functional. The residence consists of two linked pavilions, one facing the rocky hillside and meadow, the other with a breathtaking view of the forest and river. The dark walls and unexpected geometries of the interior create a space that is immersive and protective, and plays constantly with perspective.

In the living room, a bold couch and a bright custom carpet by Esther Stewart are marvels of contrast, as is the lighter, brilliantly tiled bathroom. Every art object and piece of furniture in the interior is an homage to the contemporary Australian art and design scene, with pieces by Anna Varendorff, Ebony Truscott, Kristen Perry, Fred Ganim, and Grant Featherston, making Slow Beam a unique place for interdisciplinary cultural dialogue.

Perhaps it is this conversation between art, architecture, and nature that constitutes much of Hobart House's allure. Hearth Studio's choice of textures, materials, and colors was inspired by the surrounding landscape, and the space they created became, in turn, an inspiration to its owners and the artists they commissioned.

LEFT PAGE The geometric pattern of the carpet continues the proportions established by the exterior of the residence. RIGHT PAGE The location is idyllic, with the natural beauty of the reserve providing a serene and peaceful setting for the home.

LEFT PAGE The subdued colors and clean lines create a sense of sophistication and elegance, providing a suitable backdrop for displaying works of art. RIGHT PAGE Daily activities, such as cooking, eating, or relaxing, are enhanced by the presence of the natural world.

LEFT PAGE The bright and contrasting colors of the furniture by modern Australian designers create a playful and energetic atmosphere.
RIGHT PAGE The use of a more restrained color palette in the kitchen design does not detract from its elegance and magnetism.

LEFT PAGE At night, numerous lamps fill the house with warm golden light, creating a cozy and inviting atmosphere. RIGHT PAGE A free-standing fireplace enhances the ergonomics and functionalism of the house, adding a touch of rustic charm and warmth to the space.

A SYMBOL OF A FUNCTIONALIST FUTURE

Edith Farnsworth House

LUDWIG MIES VAN DER ROHE
PLANO, IL, USA 1951

Designed by modernist icon Ludwig Mies van der Rohe, Edith Farnsworth House—a single-room home situated on the banks of the Fox River in Plano, Illinois—is a masterpiece of radically simple, unadorned architecture, and a superb example of International Style. Completed in 1951, the house was occupied briefly by its initial owner and namesake, celebrated research physician Dr. Edith Farnsworth, and its reputation in the architectural world has remained constant. Although today it is recognized as a National Historic Landmark and a destination for pilgrims of modern architecture, the home was actually built for a more modest purpose: it was intended as a secondary residence for Farnsworth, where she would be able to recharge and explore her hobbies—playing the violin, translating poetry, and enjoying nature.

Elevated 5.2 feet (1.6 meters) above a flood plain by eight wide steel columns, the structure seems to float slightly above the ground. The pavilion's spatial dimensions resemble the pavilion Mies van der Rohe created for the International Exposition in Barcelona in 1929. However, more than 20 years later, the floor-to-ceiling glass walls overlooked not the crowds in Barcelona but the solitary fields and banks of the Fox River. The entrance is designated by two sets of wide steps, connecting the ground to the deck and porch. Naturally, the material choice was limited to the mass-produced essentials typical of International Style—steel, concrete, natural stone, and glass. The house's stillness is juxtaposed with the rhythms of the natural surroundings, the subtle movements of light and shade, water, trees, bushes, and grass.

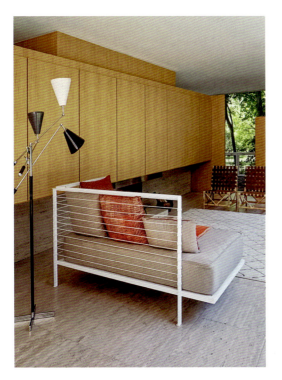

The interior provides one of the earliest examples of what was later recognized as Mies' signature concept of "universal space." Inspired by the multifunctional halls of industrial exhibitions at the turn of the 19th century, the concept treated a living or public space as a fluent and flexible single structure without walls or borders, and able to accommodate different uses. Farnsworth House's transparent, open pavilion—a single large room—contains multiple zones for sleeping, cooking,

LEFT PAGE The raised foundation of this house not only protects against the threat of floods but also gives the impression of a building that is floating or levitating.
RIGHT PAGE Wooden blocks divide the space into functional zones.
FOLLOWING PAGES The furniture currently exhibited in the house is also designed by Mies van der Rohe.

dressing, eating, and sitting, all differentiated by functional furniture. The space is also shaped by two wooden blocks, one housing the wardrobe cabinet and the other a kitchen and bathroom.

Edith Farnsworth lived in the house during the 1950s and '60s, decorating it with pieces by Scandinavian, American, and Italian modernist designers (including Florence Knoll, Jens Risom, Bruno Mathsson, and Franco Albini) who

followed the approach of clean lines and precise geometries. In 2021, within the framework of the exhibition Edith Farnsworth Reconsidered, the original decor of the house was restored in accordance with old photographs by Hedrich Blessing, André Kertész, and Werner Blaser. For instance, the main living area was concentrated around a wood dining table with white metal legs and a black and white geometric rug supported by two lounge deckchairs. In contrast, a glass desk with crossed legs appeared as a focal point in the office zone.

In 1972 the house was sold to Peter Palumbo, a British property magnate, art collector, and architecture enthusiast. With the new owner, the primary function of the residence changed, transitioning from a living space to an exhibition space. Palumbo brought in furniture Mies designed in the 1930s and works from Mies' grandson Dirk Lohan in addition to sculptures by Andy Goldsworthy, Anthony Caro, and Richard Serra.

Since 2004, the house has been open to the public as a museum, and has been visited by over 100,000 people. The museum's permanent collection and temporary exhibitions explore the remarkable history of this home, which continues to inspire architects, artists, designers, and collectors with its timeless minimalist aesthetic.

Edith Farnsworth House is a masterpiece of radically simple, unadorned architecture, and a superb example of International Style.

An Architectural Poem
of Light and Lines

May's Point is an architectural achievement that reflects the surrounding nature, which in turn reflects a state of mind. Created by Tanner Architects, this coastal pavilion is breathtaking and picturesque, yet ergonomic down to the tiniest detail. A hidden gem of the South Arm Peninsula, the house offers deep contact with the setting—contact whose intensity can be adjusted based on its inhabitants' desires. The house currently provides a second home to a Sydney-based family of five, and its location on a peninsula has provided the perfect locale for generations of surfers.

The structure, an architectural poem of light and lines, rises up from the rolling shoreline of Opossum Bay. When viewed from the house, the horizon seems to constantly shift, as does the extraordinary Tasmanian light. The minimalist terrace, complete with outdoor fire pit, enables a spellbinding conversation with the seascape.

Inside, the Scandinavian approach continues. Here, the primary function of the perfect geometry, accentual furniture, polished stone, and directed lighting is to highlight whatever perspective or mood the weather might bring. Despite this supporting role, interior objects have been chosen for their aesthetic beauty as much as for their functionality. The decor, with its velvety fabrics and darkly-colored shades, provides style and comfort, and imbues the interior with heightened drama.

Just as Mies van der Rohe's constructions tell us so much more about architecture than all the Bauhaus textbooks combined, this modernist pavilion has much to say about the South Arm Peninsula on which it is built. In order to capture the natural rhythms of the grassy hills and stony beaches, the moss and primeval dwarf shrubs, the designers utilized only essential materials: concrete, metal, stone, and wood. This has allowed May's Point to become, as it were, an integral part of the coastline, a coastline shaped exclusively by the forces of nature.

LEFT PAGE The expansive views and access to fresh air create a sense of
openness and freedom, inviting the sea breeze and natural elements into the space.
RIGHT PAGE Accent furniture and design pieces add lightness and playfulness.
FOLLOWING PAGES The dynamic and ever-changing sea landscape provides
a constantly shifting play of light and shadow in the interior.

The natural light enhances the elegance, beauty, and functionality of the space. RIGHT PAGE The stunning beauty of May's Point is magnified at sunset, as the golden light of the setting sun illuminates the clean lines and minimalist aesthetic of the design.

A Transformable Fortress on a Nordic Islet

WEEKEND HOUSE STRAUME   KNUT HJELTNES ARKITEKTER
REMØY, NORWAY   2016

Although it might be difficult to believe, Weekend House Straume, situated on the rocky islet of Sildegarnsholmen, came from humble origins. In designing this home, Knut Hjeltnes Arkitekter had the peculiar challenge of recreating the spatial structure of an old warehouse that had been washed away by an intense storm in 1992. The islet has belonged to the family of the house's current residents—Peter and Marianne—for many generations, hence their interest in making a permanent home there.

Designed for a harsh, flood-prone environment, the house is now equipped to survive any disaster. Seven steel frames that give the structure its shape are firmly anchored to a concrete-plinth cast, built on the warehouse's old stone foundation. Susceptible to flooding, the ground floor contains both insulated and uninsulated spaces—a kitchen and living room, plus storage for wet suits, fishing nets, and sails—fortified by steel and glass walls. Living quarters—four bedrooms, two bathrooms, and a cinema room—are located on the floor above. For extra privacy, the architects divided this level into two independent spaces, each with its own staircase. The light-filled, visually stunning attic provides extra room for storage, guest accommodation, and social events.

A feature that perhaps brings Weekend House Straume closer to a castle or fortress is the timber façade—its combination of hinged and sliding panels allows the home to, on short notice, shield all windows and open spaces, and block out the strong winds. When the residents are home, or when the weather is calm, the house easily opens back out to the world.

It is easy to imagine that the interior of such a space might include only the bare essentials. However, the house's amenities, although minimalist in nature, evoke comfort more than pure function. The spacious sofa in front of the fireplace offers a ground-level spot from which to contemplate the horizon and listen to the sounds of the sea. And the wooden textures and muted colors of the bedrooms effortlessly create an atmosphere of calm and coziness.

LEFT PAGE The interior is characterized by simplicity and minimalism. RIGHT PAGE Built with seven steel frames and wrapped in a timber envelope of sliding panels, the building can remain completely anonymous when not in use, but transforms when inhabited. FOLLOWING PAGES An ascetic interior is cozy and comfortable, providing the necessary features for a functional and enjoyable living space.

LEFT PAGE The inclusion of a built-in fireplace in the interior design of a space adds a sense of warmth and comfort. RIGHT PAGE The colors and textures complement and enhance the wooden shades, creating a cohesive and harmonious aesthetic. FOLLOWING PAGES This unique building was constructed entirely off-site and transported to its final location via a crane vessel.

On a Lush, Quiet Island in the Sound

WHIDBEY FARM MWWORKS
WHIDBEY ISLAND, WASHINGTON, USA 2019

The coastal areas of the Pacific Northwest are known for their lush, majestic forests and the astonishing variety of marine life thriving in their interconnected waterways. Situated on

Whidbey Island (part of the famously beautiful Puget Sound) at the edge of a dense evergreen forest, Whidbey Farm is a part-time residence, retreat, and workplace for a large family, whose connections with the island stretch back many generations. As with all their projects, Seattle-based studio mwworks developed the residence using principles of sustainability, ecological balance, and inclusive design.

In addition to the forest, the main house also overlooks the owner's cattle-grazing fields, older buildings, and a lovely pond. During construction, it was both the architects' and clients' desire to refrain from interfering with the natural landscape; they successfully preserved Douglas firs, hemlock, and Pacific madrone, which became part of the house's visual identity. The exterior employs natural textures and muted color palettes, combining naturally aged wood, stone, and concrete with beautifully framed glass walls, and the effect feels both rustic and decidedly modern. This balance between styles seems a perfect metaphor for the house's primary purpose—to bridge the gap between generations by providing a place for meaningful memories and connections.

Various life-needs are divided between the different volumes, connected by a raised wooden walkway and path through the garden. The kitchen, dining room, and living room belong to the southern, terraced volume, which is adjoined by another volume housing the main and guest bedrooms, basement wine cellar, and laundry room. A third building holds a garage and extra sleeping and dining quarters for the guests.

The interior foregrounds the connection to the family's history. For instance, carved cedar slabs crafted several decades ago by the family patriarch (a young doctor at the time) now function as doors or wall art, while a new uncarved cedar piece in the main bedroom awaits this generation's contribution.

LEFT PAGE The inviting space is the perfect blend of farmhouse charm and modern style. RIGHT PAGE The use of local materials adds a sense of harmony and connection to the surrounding landscape. FOLLOWING PAGES Perched on a low hill, the house offers stunning views of the surrounding landscape, including nearby cattle fields, a picturesque pond, and the lush forest itself.

LEFT PAGE Natural wood finishes to cozy furniture and charming accents, every detail of this farmhouse-inspired space exudes warmth and sophistication. RIGHT PAGE The open floor plan allows for easy flow between the living, dining, and kitchen areas, making it the perfect space for gathering with loved ones.

LEFT PAGE At Whidbey Farm, the simple pleasures of country life are elevated to an art form, offering a taste of rural living at its finest. **RIGHT PAGE** The farm's landscape design is a blend of native plants, water features, and stone accents.

Reflecting the Beautiful Ways of Nature

LOS TERRENOS   TATIANA BILBAO ESTUDIO
MONTERREY, MEXICO   2016

Every project by acclaimed Mexican architect Tatiana Bilbao has its own distinct style, but all are united by a similarly thoughtful approach to design. In addition to their striking beauty, her projects are marked by an interest in sustainable development and a hyper-attentiveness to place. Los Terrenos—a private secondary home in the city of Monterrey, Mexico—is no exception. Making stunning use of mirrored-glass exteriors, the house has the power to reflect and mimic every detail of surrounding flora and fauna, forging a powerful connection with the landscape.

Los Terrenos is situated on the forested highland overlooking the city. Two structures, each with its own particular mood and function, surround an outdoor space that shelters a swimming pool. The mirror-covered volume is an airy, multi-zonal space containing a living room, kitchen, and dining area. From the inside, the glass walls are completely transparent, allowing residents the opportunity to contemplate nature while remaining unseen. Two private bedrooms, with raised platform beds that offer a dramatic perch from which to view the forest, belong to the second, L-shaped building. In the spirit of embracing the natural environment, the design preserved all existing trees on the site, even making space for them within the geometrical terracotta pavement.

Although it is a private residence, surely there's no harm in fantasizing what it might be like to spend the weekend at Los Terrenos. The house seems perfect for an introspective day inside, perhaps with a book in the chic bathtub, or to admire the birds and tree-tops through the transparent roof from the comfort of the plush living-room sofa. But fantasies aside, one thing is certain: Los Terrenos is in deep dialogue with its surroundings—so much so that it has managed to almost completely blend in.

LEFT PAGE The intricate textures of natural wood in the bedrooms create a sense of serenity and comfort, inviting one to relax and unwind. RIGHT PAGE The walls of the sleeping quarters are expertly crafted from rammed earth and clay bricks. FOLLOWING PAGES The social area is encased in a mirrored glass envelope that both reflects and encloses the verdant landscape outside.

LEFT PAGE The architecture allows the beauty and diversity of the
natural landscape to enhance the design. RIGHT PAGE The larger
of the two completed buildings features a spacious social zone that
includes a double-height open-plan living room, dining area, and kitchen.

LEFT PAGE The design encourages a fluid, indoor-outdoor lifestyle.
RIGHT PAGE The room is flooded with natural light and features hinged doors that can be swung open to seamlessly connect the interior with the adjacent shaded terrace.

LEFT PAGE Each room features a stepped configuration and is equipped with a retractable glass façade, allowing the space to be opened up to the outdoors and blurring the boundaries between the interior and exterior. RIGHT PAGE The two bedrooms and accompanying bathrooms in the building are thoughtfully positioned to take advantage of the varying views from the site.

LEFT PAGE Warm, ambient light inside creates a cozy and inviting atmosphere. RIGHT PAGE The wooden surfaces and textures are a subtle yet impactful design element that enhances the overall sophistication and luxury of the residence.

An Eco-Conscious Sanctuary in a Rainy Nature Reserve

RAIN HARVEST HOME   ROBERT HUTCHISON ARCHITECTURE & JSA ARQUITECTURA
TEMASCALTEPEC, MEXICO   2020

The Rain Harvest Home, a stylish and innovative residence designed by Seattle-based architect Robert Hutchison (in collaboration with local firm JSa Arquitectura) for his family, is situated in

the picturesque mountain city of Temascaltepec, 93 miles (150 kilometers) west of Mexico City. As part of the 450-acre (182-hectare) Reserva el Peñón nature reserve, Rain Harvest Home is devoted to the concept of sustainable living, with a particular emphasis on water conservation. The residence features a sophisticated rainwater collection system, which is the cornerstone of the house's design and makes the place completely water-autonomous. It also includes a bio-agriculture garden and orchard, allowing residents to harvest much of their own food.

The 4,000-square-foot (372-square-meter) residence is a harmonious blend of rustic and modern design elements, with a focus on maximizing the connection between interior and exterior spaces. Inside the house, the atmosphere is warm and inviting, with untreated timber surfaces and volcanic stone accents adding to the rustic charm. The interiors are flooded with natural sunlight, highlighting the beauty of the materials and creating a vibrant and lively atmosphere.

The furniture has been carefully chosen to complement the house's perfect balance between form and function, creating a space that is both visually stunning and practical. The living area, with panoramic windows and cozy sofa, is the perfect spot for relaxing and enjoying the beautifully lush landscape. One of the most unique features of the residence is the circular bathhouse. This building serves as both a hot bath and steam shower, with a central plunge pool and circular window in the roof that lets the rain in and provides plenty of natural light to the space, inviting relaxation and rejuvenation.

The Rain Harvest Home is a visionary project that points the way towards a more sustainable future for residential architecture. This combination of beautiful design, functionality, and eco-consciousness makes it a true haven for those seeking a more sustainable way of living.

LEFT PAGE The Rain Harvest Home is a stunning example of sustainable design of which nature is an integral part. RIGHT PAGE The clean, modern lines of the home's architecture are a beautiful complement to the surrounding landscape. FOLLOWING PAGES The residence is nestled in a lush, natural setting, surrounded by trees and greenery.

LEFT PAGE The bathhouse is a serene and peaceful space that features a hot bath, steam shower, sauna, and washroom that surround a central cold pool. RIGHT PAGE The furniture is carefully chosen to complement the minimalist aesthetic and support the home's sustainability goals. FOLLOWING PAGES The dining area is a perfect spot to gather and enjoy the tranquility of the setting.

LEFT PAGE The outdoor living spaces are designed to foster a connection with nature. RIGHT PAGE The open-plan layout and large windows reduce the need for artificial lighting and heating/cooling systems. FOLLOWING PAGES As the sun sets and the evening cools, the terrace of the house comes alive. The outdoor fireplace provides warmth and a cozy ambiance.

The Gamekeeper's
New House

THE FIND   FOUND ASSOCIATES
COTSWOLDS, U.K.   2011

The Cotswolds, a hilly, idyllic region found in southwest-central England, is well known for both its beautiful landscapes and superb traditional residential architecture. One historic structure in the

area—an 18th-century gamekeeper's cottage—became the starting point for this stately and sprawling private residence. Found Associates, an award-winning, London-based architecture studio, renovated and extended the heritage cottage, transforming the whole site—nestled in a valley and surrounded by woods—into a striking modern living environment.

The structures added during the renovation tuck in neatly behind the gamekeeper's cottage and integrate effortlessly into the land. According to the architects, the main sources of inspiration were the rural, pastoral landscape and the architectural vernacular found in the many stone constructions of the Cotswolds. The new building is divided into three connected sections; the sharp geometrical contours of this new structure complement rather than clash with the harmonious structural features of the original Georgian architecture. Here, tradition and modernity work together in a visual ensemble.

While the exterior of the new pavilions mimics the original gamekeeper's cottage, at least in terms of its colors and surface materials, the interior breaks further from tradition, and enjoys its own contemporary, minimalist identity. Here we find a spacious, open-plan kitchen, exquisitely arranged living room, extensive fireplace (with a wood-storage area that makes ingenious use of a recessed space), and floor-to-ceiling windows showcasing the valley, nearby pond, and surrounding forests. The colors and textures of the interior create an atmosphere of lucidity and thoughtfulness, and bring the historic setting into elegant focus.

The furniture in both buildings features the same calm and light color palette, while the style differs from one space to the other—in the cottage, the shapes are soft and flowing, highlighting the coziness of the wooden elements. Meanwhile, the modernist approach of the new extension creates a more exacting and organized design.

LEFT PAGE The soft light-colored furniture harmoniously blends with the interior of the old cottage. RIGHT PAGE Modern functionality and the sophisticated splendor of 18th-century architecture are united by the stunning beauty of the southwest of England. FOLLOWING PAGES Open-plan spaces are flooded with natural light from floor-to-ceiling windows and melt into the surrounding landscape.

LEFT PAGE Towering oaks and stately beeches, rolling hills, verdant meadows, and green river bays belong to the idyllic setting of the residence. RIGHT PAGE From the original 18th-century cottage to the contemporary pavilions, every element of The Find has been carefully considered to create a unique, uplifting atmosphere.

A Fairy Tale in Warm Wood and Karelian Stone

HILLTOP HOUSE   HOROMYSTUDIO
LENINGRAD REGION, RUSSIA   2021

The climate of Russia's Leningrad region (an area in the western part of the country that includes St. Petersburg) is harsh, featuring short, damp summers and long-lasting, sunless winters with biting north winds. Yet this area, whose land borders the Gulf of Finland and two giant freshwater lakes, is cherished for its natural beauty. The trick, of course, is to find yourself a cozy, stylish spot from which to view the rugged landscape. Hilltop House, a project by St. Petersburg's Horomystudio, is exactly that.

The land has undoubtedly inspired the residence's design—even the spatial structure is based on the complex relief of the setting. The less-prominent ground floor, with its garage and storage space, seems almost an extension of the hillside, and its stairs mimic the angle of the slope. The main living area, indicated by its panoramic windows and triangle-shaped terrace with glass railings, is found on the second level. The interior is concentrated around the living room, where an epic fireplace and expansive sofa invite you to get comfortable and enjoy the views of the mixed coniferous forest. Muted colors proliferate, and the walls and floors make gorgeous use of wood and stone. The signature feature of the primary bedroom (to which the triangular deck belongs) is the freestanding designer bathtub, situated in front of a panoramic corner window.

The materials used in both exterior and interior gravitate towards those found in Nordic minimalism, but with a pinch of local tradition. The natural stone—gabbro-diabase—was sourced in the nearby Karelia region, and the darkened wood of the façade is a clear homage to Finnish rustic architecture. There are also references to Russian folk culture, such as elegant sliding shutters for the windows, with saw-cut carvings resembling traditional wooden architecture found in churches and peasants' houses. In the end, Hilltop House is every city-dweller's dream getaway: a splendid, spacious residence deep in a fairy-tale forest.

LEFT PAGE The muted tones of the interior bring incredible views of the boreal forest to the fore. RIGHT PAGE The topography of the residence's setting is characterized by its striking, curvaceous contours.

LEFT PAGE The spatial configuration of the residence is well-suited to its towering coniferous surroundings. RIGHT PAGE Natural materials, such as oak and stone, are used extensively to create a sense of connection with the untouched natural outside. FOLLOWING PAGES The interior design fosters a harmonious relationship with the surrounding environment.

LEFT PAGE Abundant natural light floods the space through large panoramic windows, creating a bright and airy atmosphere. RIGHT PAGE Traditional Russian saw-cut carving on the sliding shutters adds a rustic touch, completing the home's connection to its natural surroundings.

LEFT PAGE The design takes advantage of the hilltop location, offering a sense of elevation and connection to the natural beauty outside. RIGHT PAGE To enhance the connection with the local environment, natural materials from the Karelia region were used in the construction of this home.

High Drama and Contemplative Calm

TOFINO BEACH HOUSE   OLSON KUNDIG
TOFINO, CANADA   2016

Located on the west coast of British Columbia's Vancouver Island, Tofino is a former timber and fishing village that's become a destination for nature enthusiasts of all kinds. There are prime hikes to be found in the protected, old-growth forests, superb surfing, and even a festival celebrating the annual return of the gray whale to the region. In designing the Tofino Beach House, Seattle-based design firm Olson Kundig sought to create a structure that showcased both the intensity and drama of the ocean (as well as Tofino's often stormy weather) and the soothing, protective nature of the forest in which the home is sheltered.

Essentially composed of a single large room, the 2,500-square-foot (232-square-meter) private residence sits at the threshold between land and water. Combining light-colored wood, glass, and concrete, the house, when seen from outside, strikes the viewer as something local, even indigenous. The base of the structure has been cantilevered, allowing the forest's natural vegetation to grow beneath the home, and making it seem as though it were floating. At the same time, the minimalist design, exacting angles, and clean geometric contours clearly signal the impact of both Japanese and Scandinavian architectural approaches.

The interior is brought together by an ample, multifunctional space, combining living room and dining room. Panoramic glass walls, with views of the ocean, allow so much light to enter that you might question whether you are inside at all. Driving attention away from the landscape is the owner's art collection, which is particularly sensitive to the volume's space design. The oddly shaped wall supporting the fireplace, for example, was specifically created to exhibit a painting by Sam Francis and Diego Singh.

The Tofino Beach House is a marvel of lucidity and quiet beauty. Combining the natural beauty of the forest and ocean with the healing power of art, the house restores energy to the body and puts the soul at ease.

LEFT PAGE The design is perfectly suited to the rugged coastal environment, providing breathtaking views of the ocean. RIGHT PAGE The architecture captures the intensity and drama of the ocean, as well as the soothing nature of the forest. FOLLOWING PAGES The beach house is essentially one open, airy space, with the focus on fostering a deep connection to the ocean and the surrounding forest.

A Family's Evolving Architecture

CABIN AT LONGBRANCH   OLSON KUNDIG
LONGBRANCH, WA, USA 1959–2014

It is always thrilling when an architect designs a house for another architect—but even more so when they design a residence for themselves. And if this residence has links to the architect's ancestral past? Well, that's all the more exceptional.

The origins of the Cabin at Longbranch date back to 1912, when the grandparents of American architect, designer, and collector Jim Olson built a summer house in a forested site near Puget Sound. Although a fire eventually destroyed this structure, in 1959, while still a student, Olson designed and built his first bunkhouse on the same site, financed by a gift of 500 dollars from his father. This first 200-square-foot (19-square-meter) bunkhouse paved the way for multiple renovations and remodels over the years, with each new project integrating and expanding upon the previous builds—the most recent occurred in 2014.

The evolution of the cabin, from its humble origins to its current role as spacious secondary home for Olson, is a story of persistence and slowly unfolding brilliance. The 1980s saw it expand from its bunkhouse beginnings to three linked pavilions, while in 2003 a roof was added to connect the structures. Consciously muted colors of the exterior consecrate the breathtaking surroundings, and several mature fir trees have been integrated into the design itself.

Framed by enormous windows, the interior also makes savvy use of plywood and recycled boards, and the supporting steel beams are the same inside and out—all contributing to a feeling of unbroken connection between the house and the forest outside. Although Olson originally designed the bunkhouse as a meeting place for friends, it now serves as a creative retreat for the architect, and a place where successive members of Olsen's clan come to gather. It is a locus for generational connection and memory, perfectly expressed by the sensitively evolving architecture.

LEFT PAGE The cabin's subdued color palette and minimal use of texture allows the natural beauty of the forest to take center stage. RIGHT PAGE Over the years, the project has undergone numerous expansions, starting with a 200-square-foot (19-square-meter) bunkhouse built in 1959.

LEFT PAGE The colors and textures of the material reflect the shades of the Northwest sky and the forest. RIGHT PAGE The rooms form a single, cohesive structure that is anchored to the hillside and extends out over the surrounding landscape. FOLLOWING PAGES The architecture integrates three mature fir trees, allowing them to grow and thrive within the structure.

A FUTURIST SONNET OF GLASS AND STEEL

Eppich House II

ARTHUR ERICKSON
VANCOUVER, CANADA 1988

P ossibly the most influential Canadian architect of
the 20th century, Arthur Erickson created the first
design of Eppich House II, a modernist treasure and
family home, in 1979, and saw construction completed in
1988. Commissioned by Hugo Eppich, co-founder of Ebco
Industries, a heavy machining and fabrication
company that produced equipment for min-
ing and aeronautics, it was the second house
Erickson created for the Eppich family. Both
Eppich House I and Eppich House II are considered classics of residential modernism and
an architectural dream that finally came true.
Situated on a wooded, private estate in West
Vancouver, with a meandering creek winding
its way through the property and serving as
a reflecting pool, the four-bedroom house is a
visual symphony of curved glass and steel. The

interior of the residence spans a generous 6,000 square feet
(557 square meters) across three beautifully terraced levels,
and the architecture contains allusions to Erickson's previous
projects. The revolutionary structural design speaks volumes
about the architect's commitment to technical innovation,
yet this futuristic approach seems in deep conversation with
the landscape, creating a harmonious connection between the
two. The outcome is an aesthetic that seamlessly integrates
the built environment into the surroundings, resulting in a
truly stunning visual effect. Erickson primarily draws on
the tradition of modernist, nature-oriented residential architecture practiced and perfected by Mies
van der Rohe and Frank Lloyd Wright,
but here reaches an apogee of aesthetic
functionality all his own.

Despite being extremely original and archi-
tecturally expressive, the house is highly
sensitive to its natural surroundings. Not
only does the curvilinear spatial structure
correspond with the landscape, but the
reflective surfaces of custom-made steel
with dichromate finish offer an unconven-
tional, but ultimately perfect complement to
the environment. According to the Eppich
family, the landscape design (by German-
Canadian architect Cornelia Oberlander)
is quite well-known to the local fauna—
eagles, raccoons, and bears—who frequent
the creek and lily pond. Miraculously, the

LEFT PAGE The house
has a pavilion-like
appearance, with clean,
geometric forms and a
strong connection to the
surrounding landscape.
RIGHT PAGE Eppich
House II is considered
by many to be Erickson's
most complete work, as
it showcases many of his
key design principles.

LEFT PAGE The curved steel structure elements were crafted by Ebco Industries. RIGHT PAGE The house is a prime example of the integration of art and architecture, with its sleek and modern design that is both functional and aesthetically pleasing.

splendor of the architecture does not detract from so much as enhance the beauty of the wooded surroundings. Consisting of a complex, yet ingeniously minimal system of glass and aluminum wall panels, punctuated by stainless-steel columns that, in turn, support white structural beams, the house bears more than a slight resemblance to a frozen waterfall, an image that has followed the house from the earliest drawings. Transparent and shimmering

walls allow the landscape views and reflections to become a significant part of the interior, coexisting with furniture and decor designed by Arthur Erickson and his life partner Francisco Kripacz, and manufactured by Ebco Industries.

Playful and chic yet comfortable and functional, Francisco Kripacz's furniture silhouettes mimic the outlines of the house. In the living room, there are chairs, armchairs, and a sofa whose shape reflects the arc at the end of the house. The primary materials of the interior objects are consistent with the house's obsession with metal and glass, but, especially with regards to the tables and chairs, they are human-scaled and quite inviting. However, the magic of the interior design is that ordinary life and everyday activities in this completely transparent masterpiece are rendered to be calm, intimate, and comfortable. This coziness is achieved through thoughtful features and details, such as the serene color palette of the bedrooms, hemlock ceilings, and multiple sources of warm light: a spacious fireplace in the living room, for example, as well as a stylish standing lamp designed by Kripacz, and silver candlesticks commissioned by the Italian silversmith Cleto Munari. The privacy of the bedrooms is reinforced by half-vault, "conservatory" spaces full of houseplants and protected by a wall of gorgeous, opaque glass blocks.

LEFT PAGE The bedroom's glass façade allows for stunning views of the surrounding trees, blurring the lines between the indoors and outdoors. RIGHT PAGE The design of the residence features multiple levels, each culminating in a semi-vaulted green space with glass blocks for privacy.

The revolutionary structural design speaks volumes about the architect's commitment to technical innovation, yet this futuristic approach seems in deep conversation with the landscape.

LEFT PAGE The landscape design of the residence, crafted by the renowned Cornelia Oberlander, provides a natural habitat for wildfowl. RIGHT PAGE At every turn, the views of the surrounding trees and water create a sense of unity between the interior and exterior spaces. FOLLOWING PAGES The architectural design resembles a frozen waterfall with a series of curved levels that cascade down the slope of the land.

A FORTRESS OF MINIMALIST SPLENDOR

Els Comellars

JOHN PAWSON AND CLAUDIO SILVESTRIN
SANTANYÍ, SPAIN   1989

Extraordinarily distinctive and original in terms of late '80s Mallorcan architecture, Els Comellars—a minimalist residence created by award-winning British architect John Pawson in collaboration with Italian master of minimalism Claudio Silvestrin—is today regarded as a classic. It was the star duo's first residential project together, and to this day, it continues to inspire architects and landscape designers with its timeless, splendid aesthetics. Located on the southern part of the island, where almond and olive groves overlook both mountains and sea, the house was commissioned by German art dealer Hans Neuendorf to create a vacation home for his growing family.

Hidden behind tall, clay-colored walls, the 1,970-square-foot (183-square-meter) villa includes a spacious courtyard, several terraces, a tennis court, and a saltwater swimming pool. The residence's architecture is a study in contradictions and contrasts, but manifests a sense of strength and impregnability through its monastic, almost defensive design—characterized by sliding windows, narrow passageways, sharp outlines, and imposingly solid exterior walls. Yet this robust façade is softened by the warmth of the prevailing pink color palette and the home's carefully considered proportions, creating a space that is both human and inviting. The residence's architects, now renowned for their expertise in interior design, have applied the principles of this discipline to the external environment as well. The system of terraces, with its carefully considered interplay of light and shadow, becomes a series of livable communal spaces even at the height of summer. The surrounding natural beauty is framed by walls and overhangs, creating a series of moving, picturesque canvases. The relationship between the residence and the natural landscape can playfully be described as "tough love." On one hand, the color and sharp contours of the façade seem designed to emphasize the beauty of the almond and olive groves and blue sky. The complex spatial structure of the building also showcases the stunning sea and mountain views, and

LEFT PAGE The façade, crafted from pink concrete, evokes a sense of both fortitude and futuristic technology, recalling the fortresses of yesteryear and the spaceships of tomorrow. RIGHT PAGE White walls emphasize the stunning views of the surrounding island, visible through every window of the house. FOLLOWING PAGES Traditional notions of interior and exterior space are merged, creating a harmonious whole.

the terraces encourage residents to spend time outside. Yet this is perhaps contrasted by the fortress-like quality of the house, which, from behind high walls, guards against the relentless summer sun and offers protection and seclusion. But it is precisely this negotiation between openness and enclosure that gives the residence its unique mood.

Inside, the building is reminiscent of the traditional stucco houses of southern Spain, characterized by ergonomics and

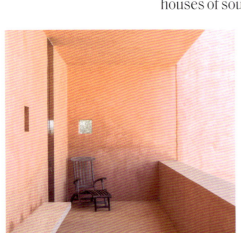

functionalism. The white palette of the interior turns it into an exhibition space awaiting its art, a blank canvas onto which visitors can project their own dreams. At the same time, the wooden furniture and abundance of daylight give a feeling of coziness and comfort. The living areas of the villa abound in with high ceilings and ample space, creating a luminous environment that exudes clarity and freshness.

Finally, the residence's imposing architectural language is counterbalanced by the laid-back atmosphere of the Mediterranean, resulting in a light and playful ambiance. This contrast creates a sense of an ongoing puzzle, a game that can never be fully solved. Despite the exterior's rigorous and exacting architectural solutions, the villa's interior is a constantly changing landscape, influenced by the movement of the sun throughout the day and the changing weather and seasons. What is accomplished by this changing light is a space that fosters thought and creativity, and the minimalist and functional design only serves to enhance this effect. The light also plays a transformative role in the exterior of the villa, altering the pink hue of the concrete façade and reflecting off the pool. These changes create a constantly shifting array of accents that play across the surface of this grand and unapologetic monolith.

LEFT PAGE In the local language, "comellars" refers to a type of shelter or enclosure, which is fitting given the protective and sheltering spirit of the house. RIGHT PAGE The contours of the pool are aligned with the architectural form, complementing the geometric proportions of the building.

The residence's architecture is a study in contradictions and contrasts, but manifests a sense of strength and impregnability through its monastic, almost defensive design.

LEFT PAGE The use of pigments from the local soil to tint the pink concrete of the façade creates a subtle connection between the building and its surroundings, bridging the gap between nature and architecture. RIGHT PAGE The house is situated within a lush landscape of almond and olive groves, providing an idyllic setting for the building.

360-Degree Living in a Mediterranean Forest

SOLO HOUSE   OFFICE KERSTEN GEERS DAVID VAN SEVEREN
MATARRAÑA, SPAIN   2017

This extraordinary holiday home is the second in a series of residential dwellings, or Solo Houses, curated by French developer Christian Bourdais, who commissioned a group of leading architects for each of the 15 projects. Located in Matarraña, a region cherished for its mountain forests, this ring-shaped house stands as an ideal example of a nature-oriented dwelling, one that embodies the best features of both modernism and functionalism. The Belgian firm OFFICE Kersten Geers David Van Severen focused on connecting these uncanny postmodernist shapes to those found in the surrounding landscape.

Behind the peculiarly shaped, single-level structure (with ample garden space at the ring's center) lies the concept of the pavilion, beloved by 20th-century minimalists. It is a bold and assertive design, yet light and free of visual excess. The total surface area is 5,250 square feet (488 square meters), and this includes 3,345 square feet (311 square meters) of patio space. The ring is divided into three main spaces—the living room and kitchen, the main bedroom, and the guest bedrooms—with movable walls designed by Belgian artist Pieter Vermeersch. The walls, spacious windows, and glass surfaces blur the boundaries between inside and out, and the house has the feeling of both hideaway and lookout. Designed to exist entirely off-grid, the house employs solar panels for heating and electricity, roof tanks for rainwater collection, and a filtration system to purify the water.

Sunbeams warm the interior to its core, reflected by every possible surface: metallic curtains, reflective bathroom enclosures, and mirrored doors. Metal and concrete textures are bolstered by pieces from Belgian studio Muller Van Severen and Brussels-based artist Richard Venlet. But in the end, this complex symbiosis of art, architecture, and design is united by one pursuit—to offer its inhabitants a singular sensory experience in the magnificent forest of Matarraña.

LEFT PAGE The choice of interior and exterior materials is mutually complementing. RIGHT PAGE The circular house almost melts into the forest, emphasizing and showcasing the natural surroundings. FOLLOWING PAGES The use of a simple circular roof with a 148-foot (45-meter) diameter draws attention to the relationship between the built and natural environments.

LEFT PAGE OFFICE has carefully curated a collection of contemporary furnishings, including work from the renowned designer duo Muller Van Severen. RIGHT PAGE The incorporation of environmentally friendly elements and the collaboration among artists has created a space that blends natural and manmade forms.

LEFT PAGE The warm wooden surfaces, bathed in sunlight, create a sense of comfort and coziness despite the minimalist decor. RIGHT PAGE Residents of the house have the opportunity to experience all stages of daily life with the stunning forest landscape as a captivating backdrop. FOLLOWING PAGES Two water filtration systems are incorporated into the roof of the building to enhance the sustainability of the site.

LEFT PAGE The house is located in Cretas, a natural and untouched forested area in the mountainous Spanish region of Matarraña.
RIGHT PAGE With curtains for added privacy when needed, almost every part of the house can be opened up to fully embrace the natural surroundings. FOLLOWING PAGES Matarraña Valley is often called "Spanish Tuscany" because of its dense forests, rolling hills, and rugged mountains.

Following Nature's Perfect Blueprint

ARCHIPELAGO HOUSE   NORM ARCHITECTS
NORTH OF GOTHENBURG, SWEDEN   2020

Not many creative movements can compete with the precision and elegant modesty of Nordic design—except, perhaps, that found in the material culture of contemporary Japan. What would hap-

pen if these two movements were combined? The Archipelago House, designed by Norm Architects, offers an answer to this question. In this project, Japanese product design and Danish architecture work in perfect synchrony.

The Stockholm archipelago provides all the beauty of the far north: deep graphite waters, strong winds, cliffs and sharp rocks, and rare trees and mosses, with rough snowy winters and mild sunny summers. It is the perfect location for solitude, rest, birdwatching, and foraging. According to Norm Architects, nature should be considered a guideline for design, rather than a simple component. That is why every architectural feature of this five-level private summer residence relies on the landscape that has been given, and never contradicts it.

The house consists of four wooden structures connected by a terraced deck. Surfaced with light wood, two of the main buildings recall traditional local architecture, and in their colors, suggest the cliffs and trees behind them. Emphatically minimalist outside, the house provides comfort, style, and functionality, while simultaneously following the dictates of the cliff-level it is built on. The muted color palette sets a calm and soothing mood throughout.

Because of the landscape-centered spatial structure, everything seems to have its unique place. All storage is hidden behind stair-cases or in the walls, leaving the main spaces empty for unen-cumbered living. In terms of accents, the Washi paper pendants and lamps were created in collaboration with Kojima Shouten—a Japanese design studio famous for its close relationship with tradition and nature.

Archipelago House merges both Japanese and Scandinavian design schools, gathering together a love of quality, functionality, ergo-nomics, and convenience.

LEFT PAGE The interior combines Scandinavian and Japanese design approaches. RIGHT PAGE Archipelago House is a collection of four pine-wood buildings that are positioned to follow the rocky terrain of the site and each of the buildings features gabled roofs that are reminiscent of the nearby boathouses.

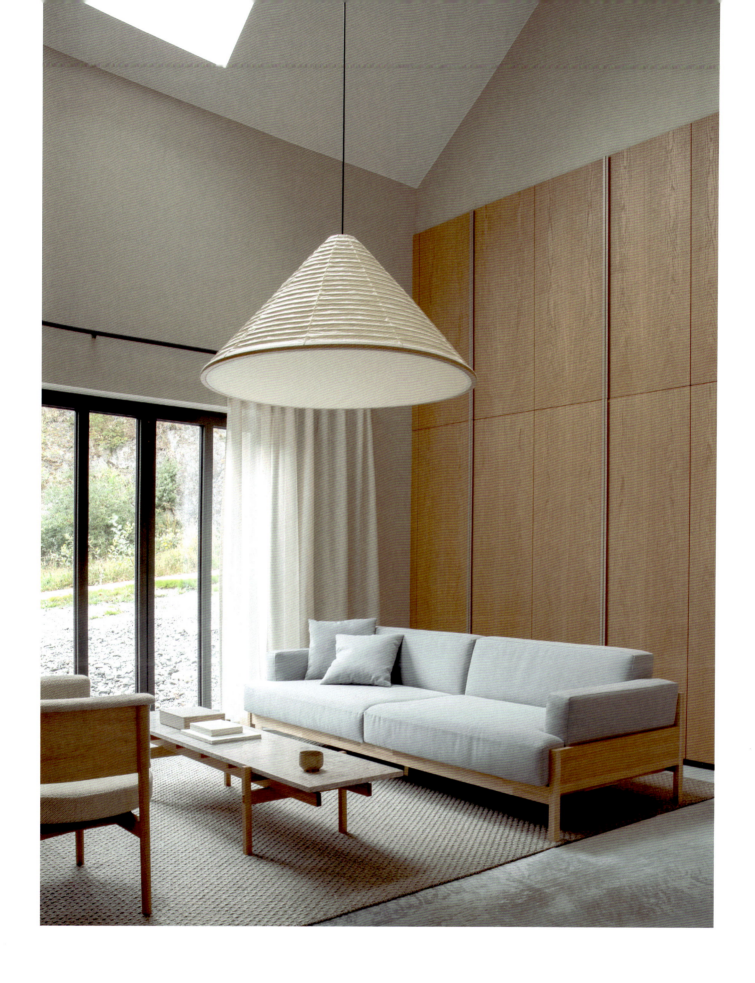

LEFT PAGE The Stockholm archipelago is known for its beautiful landscape, with its rocky shores, forests, and crystal clear waters. RIGHT PAGE The furniture is designed by Norm Architects and Karimoku Case Study, known for its high-quality, handcrafted pieces.

LEFT PAGE The double-height lounge is the central gathering space full of ample natural light. RIGHT PAGE The kitchen features handleless oak cupboards and a jet-black breakfast island with built-in drawers.

LEFT PAGE The light wood of the façades allows the buildings to merge with the Nordic environs. RIGHT PAGE Panoramic windows allow residents to feel like they are a part of the natural world even while inside the house.

LEFT PAGE A cone-shaped lantern, which was created specifically for the house by the Japanese brand Kojima Shouten, is also found in the lounge. RIGHT PAGE Even the smallest interior details are inspired by the landscape.

Modern Country Haven in the Hudson Valley

HUDSON VALLEY COMPOUND   RANGR STUDIO
COLUMBIA COUNTY, NY, USA   2017

Taking cues not only from the hilly topography, the architectural structure of the Hudson Valley Compound—by Jasmit Singh Rangr's Rangr Studio—was also inspired by the sun's path through the landscape and the trajectory of the breeze, as well as the local architecture of Columbia County, New York. Designed as a secondary residence for a young family of four, these three structures, with 8,900 square feet (827 square meters) of total surface area, complement and contextually support each other, creating an extensive outdoor communal space in between.

Despite the design's modernist leanings, the Hudson Valley Compound remains closely connected to its natural surroundings, with wall-sized windows offering views of the long lawn, rolling hills, and nearby forests (or a gorgeous snowy expanse in winter), sliding panels, and multiple terraces comfortable in any season. The spacious-yet-intimate main structure has double-height living and dining areas, seven second-floor bedrooms connected by a balcony, and two garages. Another living space, separable from the main structure when needed, contains guest bedrooms, a playroom, and another garage. The outdoor terrace, with a stunning, panoramic valley view, transitions effortlessly to the adjoining heated swimming pool, whose stone steps are a nod to ancient Indian stepwells. Nearby, a smaller separate guest house accommodates two bedrooms, a living area, and a large wrapping screen porch.

Every structure on the property is linked to the valley's landscape in its own unique way, yet all provide picturesque, idyllic views unobstructed by columns. The interior has many eclectic accent pieces—the pair of gold and crystal chandeliers over the dining room table are one example—but the atmosphere remains cozy and peaceful due to the muted color palette and light, luxurious textures (wood, marble, chrome, and tiles). Although the world outside the Hudson Valley might seem far away here, the compound is remarkably self-sufficient, minimizing its footprint by harnessing geothermal and solar energies for its primary power sources.

LEFT PAGE The design of the building, from its materials and colors to its overall form, has been carefully chosen to match the architectural style common in Columbia County. RIGHT PAGE Whether it's for enjoying a refreshing swim or simply soaking up the scenery, the pool offers an unforgettable experience.

LEFT PAGE Panoramic windows provide expansive views of the surrounding natural landscape, allowing the beauty of the outdoors to permeate every part of the house. RIGHT PAGE The space around the fireplace becomes one of the most pleasant communal areas of the home. FOLLOWING PAGES Stone steps descend from the terrace to a long pool, continuing down into the water in a manner reminiscent of ancient stepwells found in India.

A Heartfelt Manifesto for a Living House

HOURRÉ   COLLECTIF ENCORE
LABASTIDE-VILLEFRANCHE, FRANCE   2015

Collectif Encore is an architecture and landscape-design agency whose approach aims to unite one with the other. Their understanding of the possibilities and potential of certain structures is

quite specific and unique. Focused on revitalizing and reconstructing heritage architecture, Collectif Encore designs a project only after acknowledging the requests of the broadest range of participants. Following the principles of participatory architecture, the collective pays heed to the residents' needs, and is conscious of what the natural context and biosphere might require.

The Hourré is the current residence for members of the collective and it exemplifies the architects' signature style. In creating the home, they transformed a humble, 300-year-old Basque farmhouse lying in ruins into a contemporary, sparkling, and inclusive living environment with minimalistic (and often invisible) design solutions, carefully preserving the farmhouse's identity and character. Every possible element of the original design remained and was thoughtfully incorporated into the reimagined residence. Thus the space left by the farmhouse doors now frames a lovely view of Basque Country, while hammock-like netting has replaced the old fallen-in second floor, transforming the upstairs into a space for games and rest.

With interference to the farmhouse's identity kept to a minimum, the contemporary design elements bring a playfulness to the mix, creating an environment perfect for living and working together. A large, shared table in the communal area invites residents to create and collaborate, while colorfully painted doors, window frames, and ceiling beams provide unexpected shots of inspiration. With the addition of the glass roof, panoramic windows, and stylish furniture, the whole volume comes alive as a multifunctional social space. With Hourré, by occupying the role of architect and client simultaneously, and through their loving, contemporary redesign of a heritage structure, Collectif Encore has created a "manifesto for a living house."

RIGHT PAGE The home is equipped with two construction safety nets which serve a dual purpose as both protective barriers and leisurely amenities, providing an unexpected and imaginative feature that enhances the livability of the space. FOLLOWING PAGES The architects have redesigned the doors of the home to function as sliding windows that disappear when opened, enhancing the connection to the natural environment.

LEFT PAGE The architects preserved most of the original elements of the space, incorporating them into the new design in a way that adds playfulness and character. RIGHT PAGE Staircase of this old farmhouse now functions as a seating area, a viewing platform for the kitchen, and a bookshelf, among other things.

LEFT PAGE The spaces and furniture within the house are designed to be adaptable to serve multiple purposes. RIGHT PAGE The upstairs bathroom is located on an open terrace so the residents can bathe under the open sky. FOLLOWING PAGES The Hourré has a strong connection with nature, with 50% of the residence dedicated to outdoor areas.

A Coastal Play
of Sun and Shade

HOUSE ON THE SAND   STUDIO MK27
TRANCOSO, BRAZIL   2019

From its quiet, sun-dappled spot in the tropical forest of Trancoso, House on the Sand looks out toward the beach of Itapororoca and the Atlantic Ocean beyond, creating a feeling of both openness

and seclusion. Until recently, Trancoso had been a quiet fishing village, but today it is one of the region's more fashionable getaway destinations, thanks to breathtaking beaches, pristine jungle, and elegant, brightly painted dwellings. Designed by Studio MK27, whose formally elegant projects carry on the traditions of Brazilian modernism, House on the Sand offers both a heightened aesthetic experience and an immersive natural encounter.

The house's extensive wooden deck, raised ever so slightly above the sand, supports five separate, unconnected buildings. To increase the feeling of openness, only necessary spaces have been enclosed, making the communal spaces brighter and livelier. Up above, an extensive eucalyptus pergola creates a gorgeous atmosphere of filtered light and latticed shadows. Several trees growing around the site are protected by the deck and roof, providing an additional layer of shade for the inhabitants, and an overall feeling of abundance and symbiosis.

Each structure serves its own distinct purpose: as primary or guest bedrooms, spacious kitchen, or dining area. Yet the deck and roof tie everything together, further erasing the boundary between inner and outer. The residence also encompasses two microclimates—the jungle, where the house resides, and the beach, near where the swimming pool is found. In contrast to the house's geometrical silhouette, the pool has a much softer outline, practically disappearing into its surroundings. Explaining their methodology, Studio MK27 notes that House on the Sand holds a unique position among functional architecture, because "nature, light, shadows and the constant and infinite sound of the ocean become the fundamental materials of the project." Indeed, when seated beneath the pergola in the hazy shade of the afternoon, it would be impossible not to fall under the house's spell.

LEFT PAGE The high-quality furnishings and minimalist aesthetic emphasize the natural light and ocean views.
RIGHT PAGE The project occupies a site area of 70,720 square feet (6,570 square meters).
FOLLOWING PAGES The swimming pool, positioned closer to the shoreline, has a natural shape that complements the design of the house.

LEFT PAGE This unique blend of styles creates a visual aesthetic that is both modern and timeless, paying tribute to the rich cultural heritage of Brazil. RIGHT PAGE The interior features an armchair by Jean Gillon, adding a touch of luxury and refinement.

LEFT PAGE The architecture is an homage to Brazilian modernism of the 20th century with a traditional local housing approach. RIGHT PAGE A dining table was created by Roger Capron, one of the most important and influential ceramicists of the 20th century. FOLLOWING PAGES The entire deck is covered by a permeable eucalyptus pergola, providing residents with a constant source of shade.

A Minimalist House with Nothing to Hide

THE GLASS HOUSE   ROOM 11 ARCHITECTS
KOONYA, AUSTRALIA   2021

Sometimes the line between art and architecture is so thin that it becomes difficult to classify a structure—is it a functional dwelling, we ask, or is it simply a work of art? This question most certainly

arises when we consider Room 11's new project, a glass house situated on the breathtakingly beautiful Tasman Peninsula. For this project, architects Thomas Bailey and Kate Phillips, in collaboration with the building's owner, have created a bold, intuitive, and daringly open structure that investigates what it means to be authentic.

Certainly in conversation with the iconic glass pavilion of 20th-century modernist architecture, The Glass House stands out for its particular relation to the surrounding landscape. In this case, the minimalist design makes no effort to blend, and yet the neat, clean, and transparent structure seems to make itself known, even vulnerable to the location, which suggests an authenticity of a different kind. The steel framing of the roof, corners, and foundation augments the view of the peninsula when seen from afar, while the house provides a singular experience to its inhabitants: each of the four walls creates its own contemplative, slow-moving picture, as nature unfolds in real time.

Although certainly sensitive to visual aesthetics, the house doesn't skimp on the need for well-being. The architects' careful attention to the area's microclimate allowed them to design the space to be comfortable all year round, no matter the fluctuating temperatures and humidity levels—particularly important when you live in a glass house. The interior continues the minimalist approach of the exterior: it is an open space, with multiple functional zones serving as bedroom, living room, and office. The furnishings are spartan but exquisitely chosen, the wood floors fresh and welcoming. Determining whether The Glass House is art or architecture is beside the point: it is simply itself, and it is both.

LEFT PAGE Fully transparent home designed to stand alone with the enchanted landscape of the Tasman Peninsula. RIGHT PAGE The outdoor space is represented by a geometric wooden terrace that continues the contours of the house. FOLLOWING PAGES The exposed quality of the pavilion can be seen as a modern interpretation of Mies van der Rohe's iconic typology.

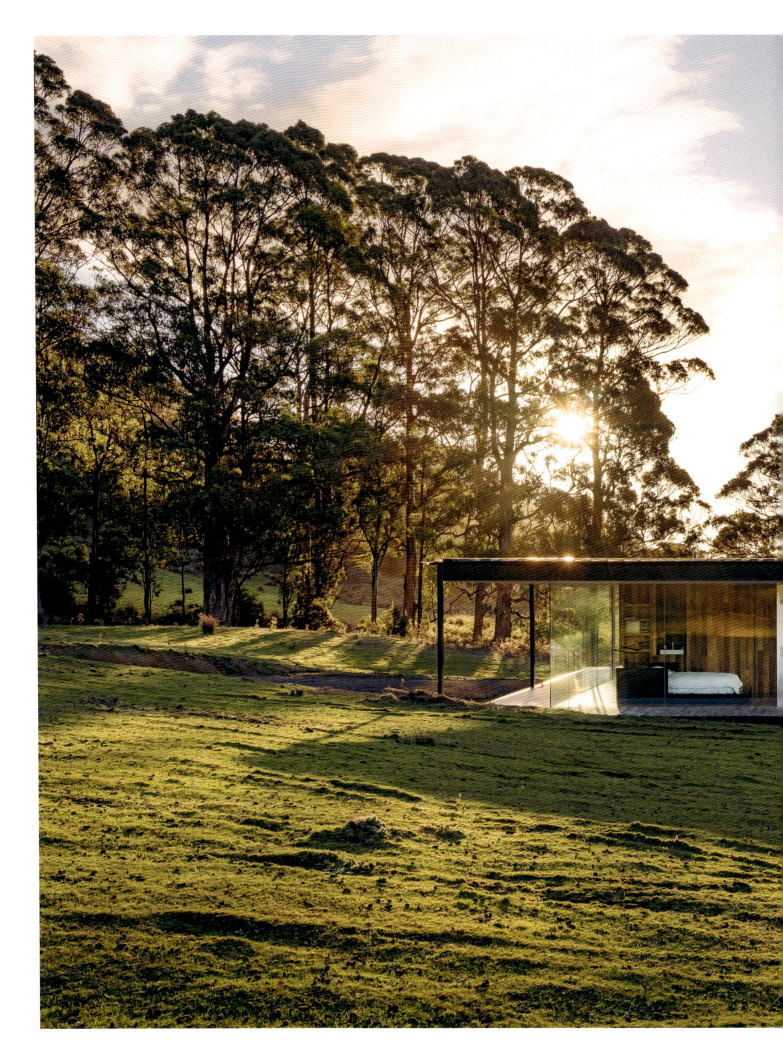

LEFT PAGE The whole interior appears as one room with designated zones marked with functional furniture. RIGHT PAGE The minimalist design draws attention to the warmth and comfort of the fireplace. FOLLOWING PAGES In its reductive and ergonomic design, The Glass House is a reflection of its breathtaking surroundings, offering an unparalleled experience of place.

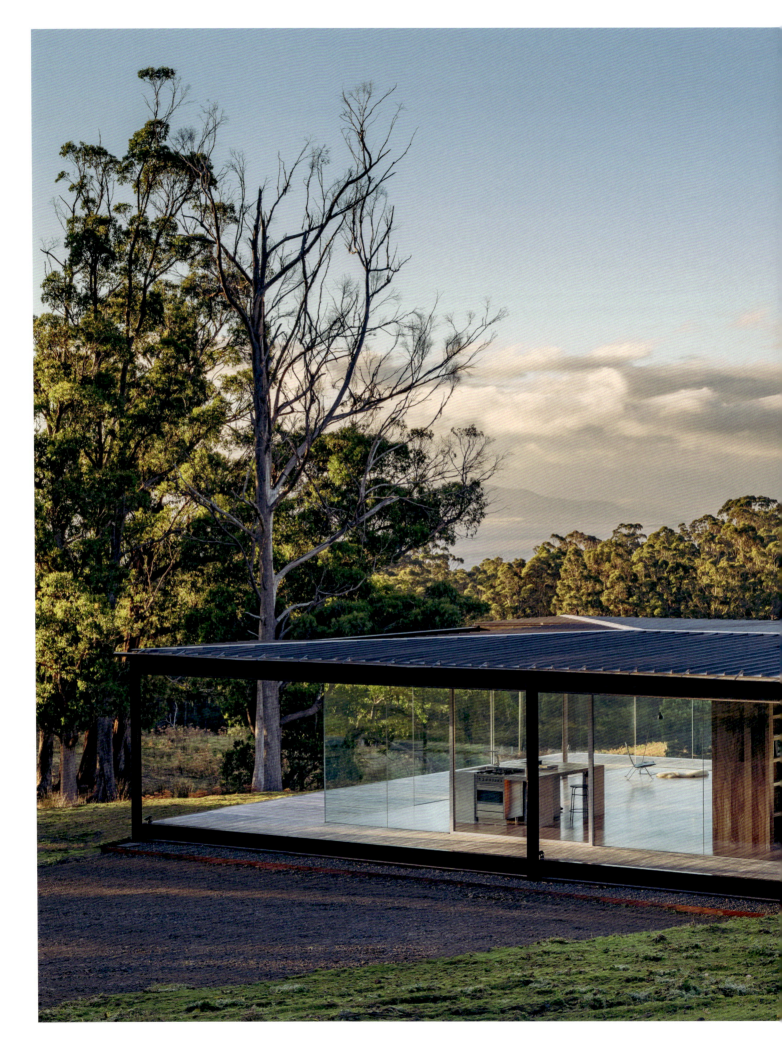

A MEDITERRANEAN TEMPLE AND HOME

Can Lis

JØRN UTZON
PORTOPETRO, SPAIN   1971

An undisputed classic of 20th-century Mediterranean residential architecture, Can Lis is perched on a cliff near the fishing village of Portopetro, on the south coast of the Balearic island of Mallorca. Renowned Danish modernist and visionary Jørn Utzon dedicated the residence to his wife Lis, and together they spent more than two decades in the house. Utzon started to work on Can Lis's design while the Sydney Opera House—undoubtedly his most famous work—was still in progress, aiming to create a home and summer escape where he could recover from his stressful and intense work on the iconic Australian project.

The Can Lis residence, rather than a single homogenous volume, is rather a collection of different pavilions and geometrical blocks connected by terraces and courtyards, with each space containing visual references to the history of the island and the oeuvre of the architect. The first cube holds kitchen and dining areas, which open up to a remarkable terrace where two flanking columns create the perfect setting for entertaining, or contemplating the dramatic ocean view. Another courtyard links to the cube-shaped living room, where a ceramic crescent-moon sofa and four low-level windows catch the sun even in winter. The moon motif is developed throughout the residence, appearing in the crescent carved out of the courtyard tiling, and in the gorgeous half-circles removed from the terrace walls. Following the contour of the cliffs, each of the five volumes faces the sea from a different angle, making the spectacular view accessible from every corner of the residence.

Can Lis inherits its spatial structure from a house Utzon intended to build in Sydney, while the corridor and courtyard system simultaneously recall the architecture of the Islamic world and the holistic spatiality of Finnish functionalist Alvar Aalto—one of Utzon's signature styles. However, the connection between Can Lis and the southern coast of Mallorca feels solid and authentic, and the house's sensitivity to its surroundings makes it feel almost uncannily natural. The primary exterior material, marés (locally sourced hard sandstone, which changes gradually from pink to

golden), resembles the color of the cliffs under the sun, and the woodwork is entirely Mallorcan pine.

The interior embraces the color and light of the Mediterranean landscape as well as traditional Mallorcan building tech-

niques. Most of the furniture—shelving, tables, chairs, and benches—was built at the site, sculptured from stone and covered with luminous ceramic tiles. Door and window openings are arranged in such a way that the daylight reaching inside is almost as bright as it is outside. Because the window frames were mounted on the exterior, they are invisible from within, and give the illusion of no boundary at all. Despite the visual minimalism and even asceticism of the interior, the house has an atmosphere of warmth and coziness. While amenities are limited to the essentials, the open, semi-linear spatial structure becomes a perfect setting for the daily routine of a family. The extraordinary supply of daylight makes one hyper-sensitive to its small changes, and connects the rhythms of the residents with the cycle of the sun's movements.

After spending 20 years in Can Lis, the Utzons moved to their next Mallorcan residence—Can Feliz—while their children continued to use the first residence for several decades. Today, the house that has set a seemingly unreachable standard for contemporary Mediterranean architecture functions as a creative residence for architects from all over the world—a collaboration between the Utzon Foundation and the Danish Architectural Foundation. Nonetheless, there is no need to have an architectural background to fully appreciate the elegance and splendor of Can Lis—like all masterpieces, its beauty is accessible, inclusive, and universal.

LEFT PAGE The kitchen furniture, illuminated by an abundance of natural light, is constructed from elegant, thin stone slabs with gleaming white tiled surfaces. RIGHT PAGE The furniture design, including the striking semi-circular ceramic sofa, was custom-made on-site.

The connection between Can Lis and the southern coast of Mallorca feels solid and authentic, and the house's sensitivity to its surroundings makes it feel almost uncannily natural.

In 2011, the Utzon Foundation restored Can Lis, transforming the space into a residence for contemporary artists. Utzon's approach to the design of Can Lis drew inspiration from Alvar Aalto's construction of the Villa Mairea, incorporating similar design principles.

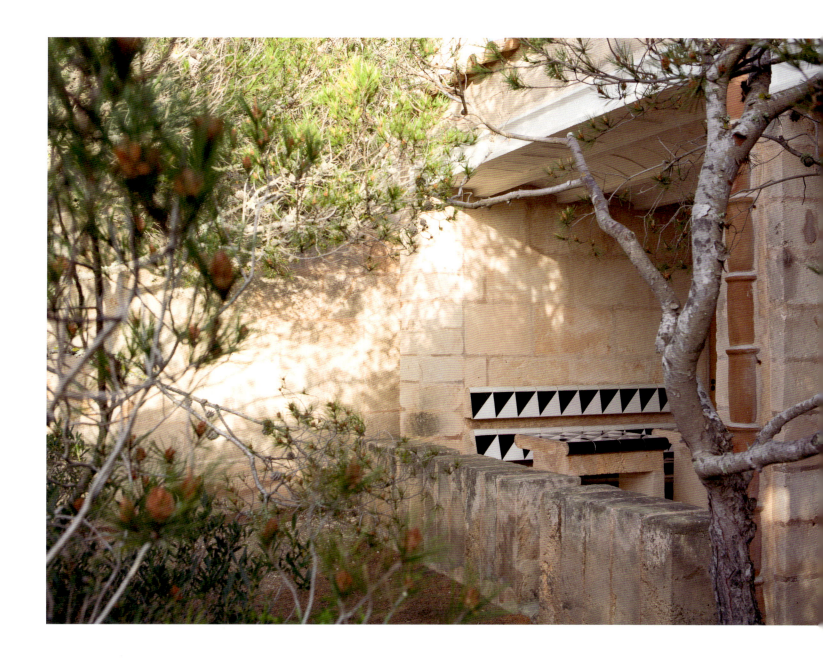

Minimalist Monolith
on the Lakeshore

HOUSE IN BRISSAGO   WESPI DE MEURON ROMEO ARCHITECTS
BRISSAGO, SWITZERLAND   2013

When imagining a lake-view residence in a small Swiss town, the last thing that comes to mind is a concrete monolith that perfectly illustrates Mies van der Rohe's principle of "Less is more." And yet this labyrinth of washed concrete, rising from the natural topography of the slope, couldn't feel more local to the shore of Lake Maggiore. Presenting the perfect balance of style and function, the bold minimalist design by Wespi de Meuron Romeo Architects allows the breathtaking landscape to play the leading part.

Following the strange logic of a labyrinth, the parking area is located on the top floor of the building, while the main entrance is accessible via a linear alleyway just beside it. The entrance courtyard door and glass front can be shifted into the wall during the warm season, allowing the exterior and interior spaces to flow together. Despite any external austerity, the interior of the House in Brissago is full of luxurious and comfortable features. Teeming with light and muted colors, the house allows for a singular, unimpeded focus on the natural surroundings. The living room, with its large panoramic window looking out over Lake Maggiore and its mountains, is perfect for social activities or isolated meditative moments.

At night, the house emanates an aura of comfort. It is surprising how much coziness and warmth are hidden beneath this concrete armor—simply light the corner fireplace, find the perfect book, and melt into the softest armchair. Most of the house's furniture seems to have been selected as much for its minimalist perfection as for comfort. An expansive heated pool highlights the terrace, but its lighting system does not outshine the moon and stars, nor their reflection mirrored in the lake's surface. However, it is in the lower-level courtyard where you experience the heart of the house. The different paths join together and give the feeling of being in an historic village—here is where the puzzle is solved. The only thing left is to relax and enjoy the view.

LEFT PAGE The addition of a corner fireplace instills a sense of coziness and luxury into the otherwise ascetic interior of this imposing monolith.
RIGHT PAGE Panoramic rectangular windows endow the interior spaces in the mesmerizing views of Lake Maggiore.

LEFT PAGE The residence's spatial structure is inspired by the logic of a labyrinth, with its winding paths and interconnected spaces. RIGHT PAGE The restrained textural palette of concrete, wood, and leather enhances the visual impact of the breathtaking landscape views. FOLLOWING PAGES The furniture adds a touch of sophistication to the space without obscuring nature.

LEFT PAGE Any spot in the house is suitable for contemplating the views of the lake. RIGHT PAGE On either side of the central courtyard, walkways and staircases descend to the expansive garden terrace, which boasts a sparkling swimming pool and outdoor kitchen. FOLLOWING PAGES In a nod to the enigmatic logic of a labyrinth, the parking area is situated on the top floor of the building.

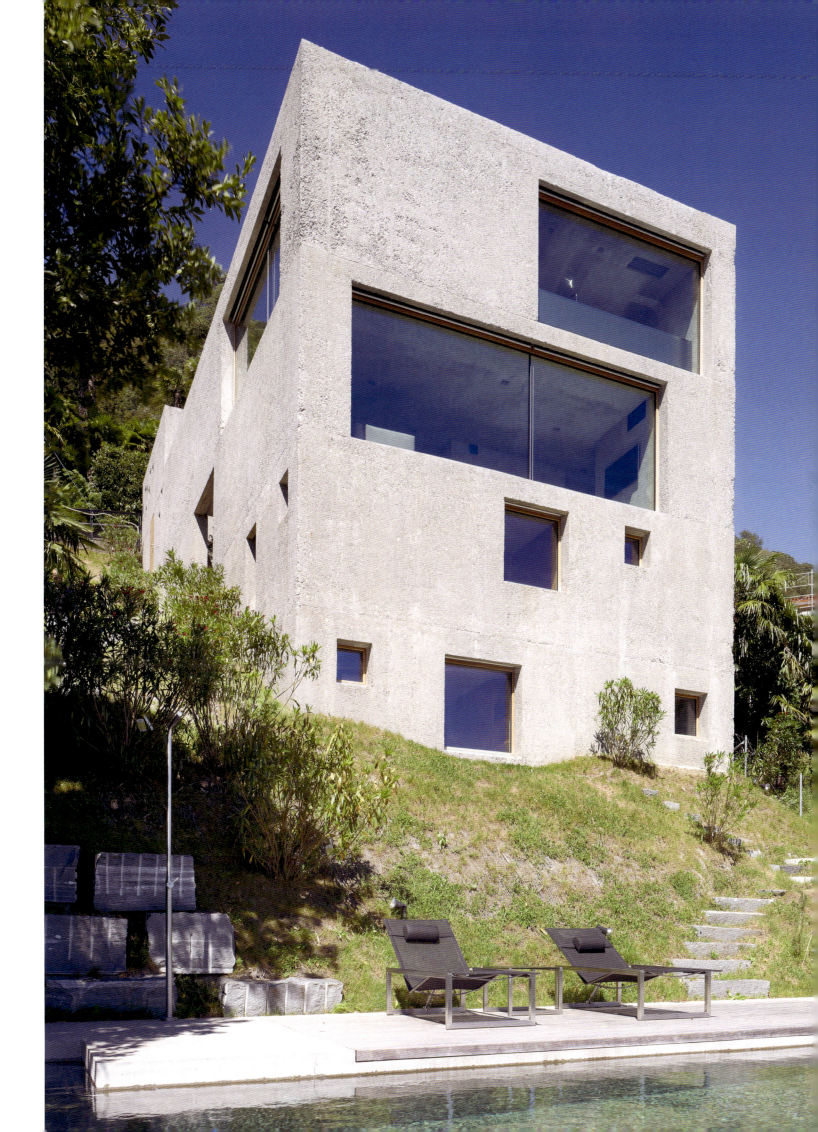

A WARM SYMBOL OF CATALAN MODERNISM

Casa Coderch

JOSÉ ANTONIO CODERCH
BARCELONA, SPAIN 1972

The renowned Catalan modernist José Antonio
Coderch finished work on Casa Coderch, his iconic
residential masterpiece and most personal project,
in 1972. At the time, the celebrated architect was at the height
of his fame, and widely considered one of the
key figures of architectural modernity. Casa
Coderch, commissioned by his sister to house
her own family, exemplifies Coderch's vision
of harmony between nature and architecture,
offering a sense of peace and thoughtful
quiet to all who enter. Nestled among pine
forests, hills, and valleys near the medieval
village of Sant Feliu de Codines, the stunning
residence is currently owned by Coderch's
nephew—Jorge Salvador. An advocate of ra-
tionalist and monumental architecture who

valued humanizing structures, Coderch created a private
and intimate family home whose design is not limited to
pure function.

Casa Coderch, built entirely from gorgeous, sun-lightened
red brick, is an irregularly shaped, open-plan residence with
a free-flowing design. Its unique spaces transform with
the changes in natural light and merge seamlessly with the
surrounding forest. The interior consists of open, airy spaces that produce a feeling of freedom. The house's layout
and use of natural materials create a sense of harmony
and unity, making it an extraordinary place to call home.
Everything here embraces the timeless beauty of nature

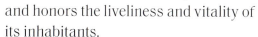

and honors the liveliness and vitality of
its inhabitants.

The 4,305-square-foot (400-square-meter),
two-story residence boasts an expansive pool, terraces, several living rooms
complete with fireplaces, and eight en
suite bedrooms—everything perfectly
proportioned and integrated. According
to Jorge Salvador, Coderch carefully re-
searched the landscape and considered
the movement of sunlight and shadows
throughout the day during the home's
construction, and this thoughtful attention to detail is evident in every part of
the property.

Casa Coderch embodies the architect's
vision of European modernity blended
with the Mediterranean culture of the

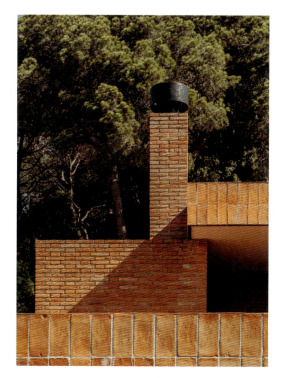

LEFT PAGE Nestled
elegantly amid verdant
pine groves and rolling
valleys, the villa stands
as an example of architectural elegance, crafted
from warm, red brick.
RIGHT PAGE Each
element of the residence,
from the contours of the
pool to the towering
chimneys, is proportioned
in relation to one another.

Catalan region. Coderch brought several decades' worth of experience working on residential architecture to the house's design, and references to many of his projects—from Casa de la Marina to Güell House—are scattered throughout the residence. In keeping with the architect's signature design elements, this home of his sister also employs a geometric, balanced, and human-scale spatial structure. The choice of materials was limited to those locally sourced or pro-

duced—terracotta bricks and natural stone, which, under the extra bright Catalan sun, seem part of the landscape itself.

In the interior, one finds a bright and minimalist design, highlighting the landscape views. The spectacular rigor and clarity of the exterior's architectural geometry is transformed here into gentle, warm spaces ideal for the quiet and calm routines of a large family. This sensitivity and attention to light and spatial rhythm is most strongly felt in the communal spaces—two living areas with fireplaces and an open terrace, where a family of 10 can dine while contemplating the landscape of the pine forests. Currently, the house's interior is decorated with furniture made of natural materials—pieces and objects Coderch initially intended to place there—creating a space that is both simple and elegant. Among these objects, hovering over a spacious corner sofa in the living room, is a famous, gourd-shaped DISA lamp, designed by Coderch himself in 1957.

Although serving as a family home for two generations, Casa Coderch has in recent years opened its doors to visitors from all over the globe, providing an extraordinary setting for a group gathering or family holiday, and a chance to live—if only for a short while—in a genuine landmark of 20th-century architecture.

The spectacular rigor and clarity of the exterior's architectural geometry is transformed here into gentle, warm spaces ideal for the quiet and calm routines of a large family.

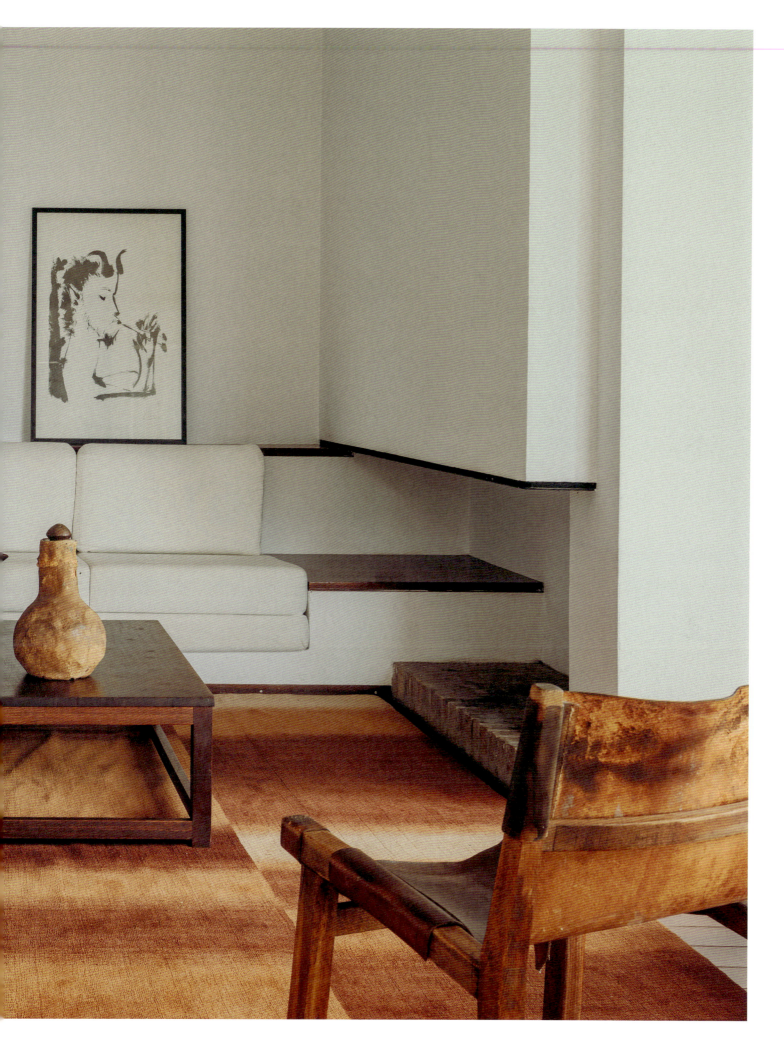

LEFT PAGE The ideal proportions and clean silhouettes of modernist architecture are in perfect harmony with the surrounding landscape, creating a balanced and visually striking environment. RIGHT PAGE Despite the delicate nature of the cladding, the geometric designs serve to contrast and highlight the beauty of Catalan landscape.

LEFT PAGE The surrounding flora has been fully integrated into the timeless architecture, becoming an inseparable part of the overall aesthetic. RIGHT PAGE With its unique blend of natural beauty and modernist architecture, Casa Coderch offers an unparalleled opportunity to immerse oneself in a world of aesthetic and peaceful serenity.

Of and Above the Ancient Atlantic Forest

CASA AZUL STUDIO MK27
GUARUJÁ, BRAZIL 2020

For the past 20 years, Studio MK27 has been leaving its mark on contemporary Brazilian architecture by cultivating a decidedly modern aesthetic. At the same time, MK27's design often draws on the nation's historical heritage, with nods toward Indigenous cultures and the Portuguese colonial era. Casa Azul is a perfect example of the studio's signature style. Staying true to its modernist beliefs down to the tiniest detail, the residence also includes some distinct Portuguese features, as if to remind us of one of the key, if controversial, influences of modern Brazilian culture.

Situated in the Atlantic Forest in the state of São Paulo, Casa Azul also lies within the environmental preservation area of Serra do Guararu. Any development in such a vulnerable location has its challenges, but Studio MK27 made it their job to impact this wild region as little as possible. The 1,312-square-foot (122-square-meter) house has a three-level structure, and is built on concrete pilotis that integrate the structure more naturally into the surroundings. On the ground level, beneath the lowest building, there is a spacious pool and sauna, and inventively shaped wooden decking that protects the concrete from excess moisture.

The living areas, whose glass doors open to transform the spaces into panoramic balconies, are located on the upper floors. Framed by elegant wooden screens (*muxarabi*) which offer sun protection without diminishing the view, the second-floor bedrooms serve as perhaps the most seductive space of the whole residence. Facing one direction, the visitor can glimpse the garden lit up by the sun, while the other offers visions of the sea and the Atlantic Forest. Both inside and out, the architects used only wood, stone, concrete, and other similarly colored textures, and this natural palette not only draws out the vivid colors of the jungle, it can make the house, at times, feel almost invisible. Although fully embracing a sophisticated modern aesthetics, Casa Azul seems equally a part of that ancient forest in which it was built.

LEFT PAGE The lush jungle landscape intervenes in the interior of the residence through the expansive panoramic windows. **RIGHT PAGE** The 1,312-square-foot (122-square-meter) house has a three-level structure. **FOLLOWING PAGES** In addition to its modern aesthetic, the residence also has some distinct Portuguese elements, signaling the influence of Portuguese culture on modern Brazilian society.

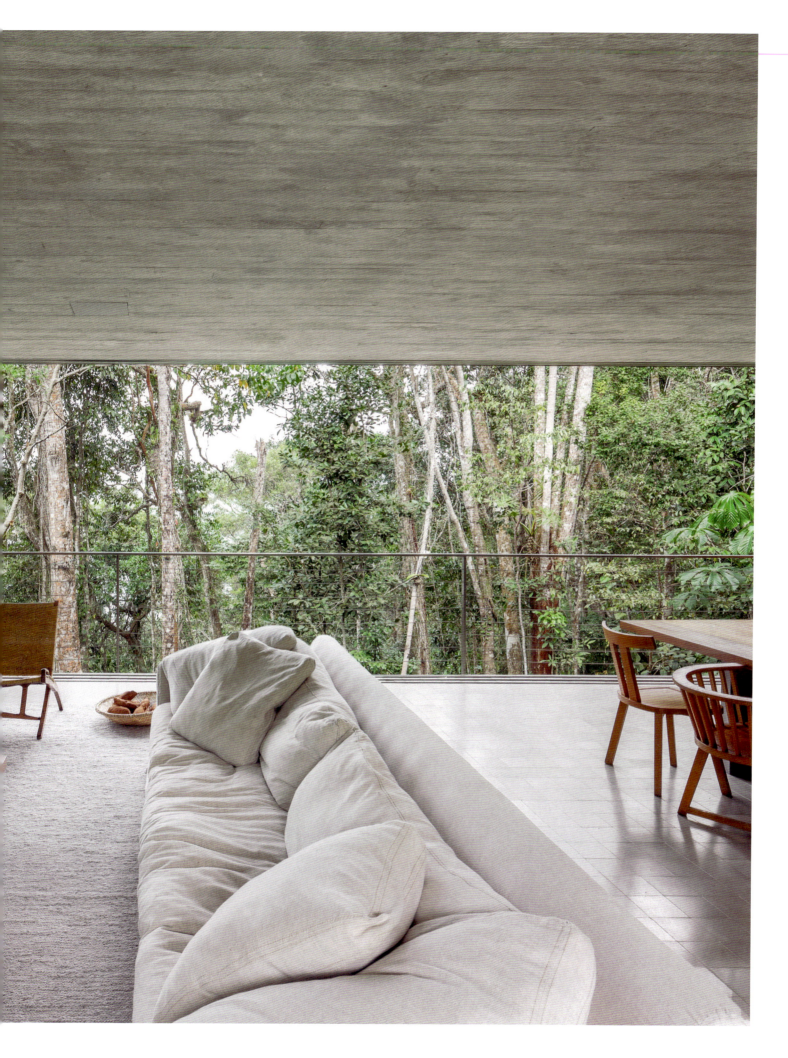

LEFT PAGE The swimming pool, partially sheltered by the deck, sits nestled between the deck and the surrounding flora. **RIGHT PAGE** The second-floor bedrooms, framed by elegant wooden screens known as *muxarabi*, provide sun protection without obstructing the stunning views. **FOLLOWING PAGES** Casa Azul fully embraces a sophisticated modern aesthetic, yet still manages to seamlessly blend into the ancient forest.

Altered State
of Consciousness

CASA SALVAJE MAZPAZZ ARQUITECTURA
PALMICHAL DE ACOSTA, COSTA RICA 2021

The idea of aligning architecture and philosophy has, through-out history, frequently been explored in government and public structures. However, the idea of applying philosophy to a private house design is still very rare. That is why Casa Salvaje—wild house—is of particular interest. While designing the residence for Costa Rican film producer and ocean conservationist Lilly Peña, Mazpazz Arquitectura integrated concepts of phenomenology, such as "perception through the senses, experiential design, and transcendence," which imbue the place with a singular thoughtfulness.

Casa Salvaje is a 394-square-foot (37-square-meter) secondary home hidden in the remote mountains of Palmichal de Acosta, Costa Rica and surrounded by cloud forests. Constructing this unique, remote, and even solitary home had its challenges—it was hard, for example, to deliver the necessary materials, equipment, and energy sources from elsewhere. But the architects thought through every detail. The house uses completely renewable energy sources—solar energy and spring water captured uphill of the house—and all the concrete, stone, and wood required for construction were produced or gathered locally.

With its imposing use of stone and concrete, and a porch whose giant circular windows create a perceptual "vortex," the house seems a distinctly Latin American take on the Brutalist tradition. Although Mazpazz Architectura wanted the house to age in such a way that it would merge into its surroundings, perhaps becoming inseparable from them, Casa Salvaje contains Brutalist features and sharp geometrical elements that constantly remind one that the "artist is present" in the forest.

Designed according to the tenets of phenomenology, the interior exercises a powerful effect on its inhabitants' consciousness. The spaces are full of natural light and calming colors, and the surface materials—marble, wood, and stone—are super tactile and pleasing to the touch. Every object seems chosen for its ability to contribute to the synergistic processes of thinking and creating. Here it seems possible to rest while traveling far in your mind.

LEFT PAGE The circular cutouts admit light and stunning views, creating a sense of movement and flow. RIGHT PAGE The house ages and blends into the jungle, becoming inseparable from its surroundings. FOLLOWING PAGES Through its carefully curated layout and use of materials, the house encourages residents to connect with their surroundings and themselves on a deeper level.

SUBLIME HIDEAWAYS

Remote Retreats and Residences

This book was conceived, edited, and designed by gestalten.

Edited by Robert Klanten and Masha Erman
Editorial support by Effie Efthymiadi

Text and introduction by Ksenia Butuzova
Text support by Michael Lee

Editorial Management by Traci Kim

Design, layout, and cover by Stefan Morgner

Photo Editor: Zoe Paterniani

Typeface: Saol by Florian Schick & Lauri Toikka

Front cover: House on the Sand by Studio MK27 (photo: Fernando Guerra)
Back cover: May's Point by Tanner Architects (photo: Adam Gibson)

Printed by Grafisches Centrum Cuno, Calbe
Made in Germany

Published by gestalten, Berlin 2023
ISBN 978-3-96704-091-3

© Die Gestalten Verlag GmbH & Co. KG, Berlin 2023

BIBLIOGRAPHIC INFORMATION PUBLISHED BY THE DEUTSCHE NATIONALBIBLIOTHEK.
THE DEUTSCHE NATIONALBIBLIOTHEK LISTS THIS PUBLICATION IN THE DEUTSCHE NATIONALBIBLIOGRAFIE;
DETAILED BIBLIOGRAPHIC DATA IS AVAILABLE ONLINE AT WWW.DNB.DE

NONE OF THE CONTENT IN THIS BOOK WAS PUBLISHED IN EXCHANGE FOR PAYMENT BY COMMERCIAL PARTIES OR DESIGNERS;
GESTALTEN SELECTED ALL INCLUDED WORK BASED SOLELY ON ITS ARTISTIC MERIT.

THIS BOOK WAS PRINTED ON PAPER CERTIFIED ACCORDING TO THE STANDARDS OF THE FSC®.